Why Science Matters

Repairing and Replacing Organs

Andrew Solway

www.heinemann.co.uk/library
Visit our website to find out more information about Heinemann Library books.

To order:
☎ Phone 44 (0) 1865 888066
▤ Send a fax to 44 (0) 1865 314091
▭ Visit the Heinemann Bookshop at www.heinemann.co.uk/library to browse our catalogue and order online.

Heinemann Library is an imprint of Pearson Education Limited, a company incorporated in England and Wales having its registered office at Edinburgh Gate, Harlow, Essex, CM20 2JE – Registered company number: 00872828

"Heinemann" is a registered trademark of Pearson Education Limited.

Edited by Andrew Farrow, Megan Cotugno, and Harriet Milles
Designed by Steven Mead and Q2A Creative Solutions
Original illustrations © Pearson Education Limited
Illustrations by Gordon Hurden
Picture research by Ruth Blair
Production by Alison Parsons
Originated by Heinemann Library
Printed and bound in China by Leo Paper Products

ISBN: 978 0 431 04070 7
13 12 11 10 09
10 9 8 7 6 5 4 3 2 1

British Library Cataloguing-in-Publication Data
Solway, Andrew
Repairing and replacing organs. – (Why science matters)
617.9'54
A full catalogue record for this book is available from the British Library

Acknowledgements
We would like to thank the following for allowing their pictures to be reproduced in this publication: © Alamy/Vario images GmbH & Co.KG p. **14**; Corbis pp. **7** (Presbyterian St. Luke's/Epa), **31** (Alessandro Di Meo/epa); © Newspix p. **46**; © PA Photos/AP p. **28**; © Photolibrary.com/Phototake Science p. **17**; © Photoshoot/UPPA p. **36**; © Photoshot/UPPA p. **20**; © Science Photo Library pp. **4** (Andrew Entwistle), **5** (Steve Gschmeissner), **6** (AJ Photo), **9** (K. H. Kjeldsen), **10** (D. Phillips), **21** (Michelle Del Guercio, Peter Arnold Inc.), **22** (Alexander Tsiaras), **26** (Eye Of Science), **27** (Kenneth Eward/Biografx), **37** (Sam Ogden), **38** (Dr Torsten Wittmann), **39** (Professor Miodrag Stojkovic), **40** (Andrew Leonard), **43** (TEK Image). Background images supplied by ©istockphoto.

Cover photograph of ears in petri dishes reproduced with permission of ©Science Photo Library (Victor De Schwanberg). Background image ©istockphoto.

We would like to thank Ann Fullick for her invaluable assistance in the preparation of this book.

Every effort has been made to contact copyright holders of any material reproduced in this book. Any omissions will be rectified in subsequent printings if notice is given to the publishers.

Disclaimer
All the Internet addresses (URLs) given in this book were valid at the time of going to press. However, due to the dynamic nature of the Internet, some addresses may have changed, or sites may have ceased to exist since publication. While the author and publishers regret any inconvenience this may cause readers, no responsibility for any such changes can be accepted by either the author or the publishers.

Contents

Some words are printed in bold, **like this**. You can find out what they mean in the glossary.

A dash through the night

It is 2.00 a.m. An ambulance speeds along just outside Buffalo, New York, USA. The ambulance contains a large plastic box. Inside is a kidney, carefully protected and packed in ice.

The kidney was removed less than one hour ago from a man who died in a road traffic accident. The operation was carried out by a medical team from a hospital in Chicago, USA. They need the kidney for a woman whose own kidneys are not working properly.

By 2.15 a.m. the ambulance has arrived at Buffalo airport. The Chicago medical team transfer to a small aircraft. In less than two hours the aircraft touches down in Chicago. An ambulance takes the kidney to the hospital. Half an hour later the kidney arrives at the hospital. It is checked carefully to make sure it is not damaged. Once the checks are completed, the operation begins.

At 9.30 a.m. the patient wakes from the anaesthetic. The new kidney has been put in place. Ten days later, she is well enough to go home. Already she feels much better than before the operation. The transplant has been successful. Although she will have to take prescription drugs and have regular checks, the woman no longer has to go to the hospital every other day.

Helicopters are useful for transporting organs. Unlike other aircraft, they can transport the organ directly from one hospital to another.

The Hartley boys

In November 2003, tests on Joshua, Nathan, Daniel, and Luke Hartley, the sons of David and Alison Hartley, showed that they had a rare disease known as **XLP** (X-linked lymphoproliferative syndrome). XLP is a disease that causes the **immune system** to respond abnormally to some **infections**. It can cause the immune system to be either underactive or overactive. Without treatment, all four boys would die before they were adults. The only effective treatment for the boys was a bone marrow transplant. Bone marrow is spongy material found in the middle of some bones. All the body's blood cells, including the white blood cells that fight off disease, are made in the bone marrow. Bone marrow cells from a healthy person would help the boys' immune systems to work properly.

Bone marrow transplants are not simple. The bone marrow has to be similar to the marrow of the person having the transplant and finding a good match can be difficult. David and Alison Hartley made an appeal for bone marrow donors through the newspapers and television. Within eight months, matching donors had been found for all four boys. The bone marrow transplants gave the boys a good chance of survival.

This electron microscope photo shows human bone marrow. Red blood cells (red) and white blood cells (blue) can be seen growing among the bone marrow fibres.

Organ shortage

Transplants of organs such as kidneys, hearts, and bone marrow can save the lives of many people with serious illnesses. However, there are far more people wanting organs for transplant than there are organs available for transplanting. As a result of this problem, thousands of people die each year waiting for a transplant.

In this book we will look at the ways in which scientists and doctors are tackling the challenge of repairing and replacing organs and other body parts, and find out how they are addressing the organ shortage. Sometimes, when an organ is damaged or goes wrong, it is possible to repair it. Recent medical discoveries may make it possible to repair more organs in the future. Some researchers are trying to improve the way that donor organs are stored. This would make it possible to keep them longer, and could make far more organs available for transplant.

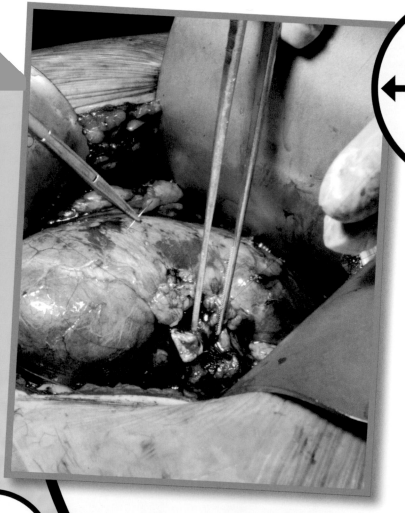

A kidney transplant operation in progress. The donated kidney is being sutured (sewn) into place.

Other researchers are trying to avoid shortages altogether by making or growing completely new organs. It may even be possible to replace a damaged organ with one transplanted from another animal.

Underpinning even the newest research and ideas is the science we learn in school. In this book we will also see how what we learn about cells, **tissues**, organs, and genetics connects to the ways that doctors save lives using organ repairs and transplants.

Organ donors

Without organ donors, no organ transplants can take place. Most donors are people who have agreed that parts of their body can be used for transplants after they die. In some countries, people must agree to becoming an organ donor, while in other countries the law is that anyone's organs may be used for transplants, unless the person has specifically stated that they do not want this to happen.

In a few cases, organs or body tissues can be taken from live donors. Humans normally have two kidneys, but we can manage perfectly well with only one. It is therefore possible for someone to donate a kidney to be used in transplantation. Usually this happens when a relative or a close friend of someone who has kidney disease offers to donate a kidney. Bone marrow can also be donated by live donors.

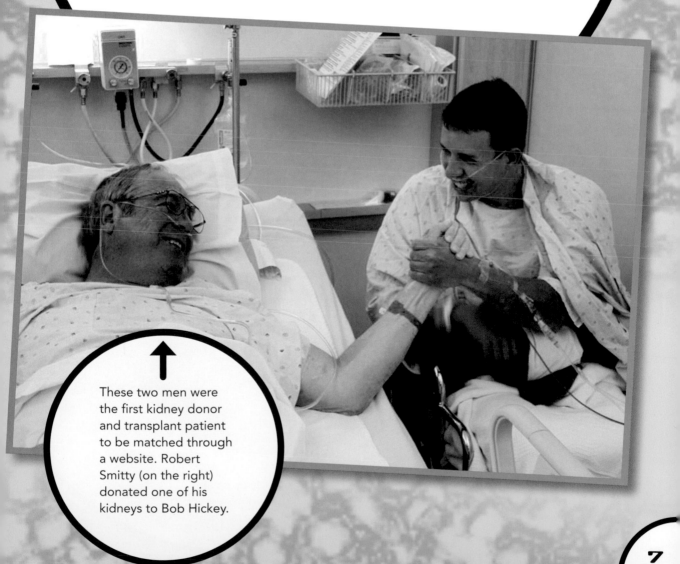

These two men were the first kidney donor and transplant patient to be matched through a website. Robert Smitty (on the right) donated one of his kidneys to Bob Hickey.

How the body is organized

Our bodies are carefully organized. Each part of the body, from the cells up, does a particular job, and each part works to support the seven life processes. The parts also work together to make the body function as an individual.

Cells

Cells are the smallest units in the body. Each cell is a tiny drop of liquid inside a thin cell membrane. Within the cell there are even smaller structures called organelles. The cell is a minute chemical factory, where hundreds of different chemical processes happen. Respiration takes place inside cells. This is the process by which sugars are broken down into carbon dioxide and water, to give the body energy. Two examples of organelles are the nucleus, which contains the genes, and the mitochondria, where respiration takes place.

This diagram shows the structure of a human cell. There are more than 75 million million cells in an adult human. →

Cell Membrane

Ribosome

Endoplasmic reticulum

Mitochondrion

Lysosome

Nucleus containing chromosomes

Free Ribosomes

Centriole

Golgi complex

Cytoplasm

Amazingly, every human starts off as just one cell – a fertilized egg – inside their mother's womb. The egg cell grows by dividing. The single cell divides into two, the two cells divide into four, then eight, and so on.

INVESTIGATION: LOOKING AT CELLS

This is a simple way to make your own slide of human cells, taken from inside your cheek. Cheek cells are non-specialized **epithelial** cells.

Equipment
- clean, wooden ice lolly stick
- microscope slide
- methylene blue dye
- cover slip
- pencil
- microscope
- paper

Procedure
1. Scrape one end of the ice lolly stick across the inside of your cheek. This will scrape some cells off the surface.
2. Wipe the end of the lolly stick on the centre of a microscope slide.
3. Add one drop of methylene blue dye to the material on the slide.
4. Carefully lower a cover slip over the drop on the slide. Use the end of a pencil to help lower the cover slip.
5. Put the slide under the microscope on low magnification. Move it around until you find some cells. Now change to a higher magnification.
6. Look carefully at the cells, and draw what you see.

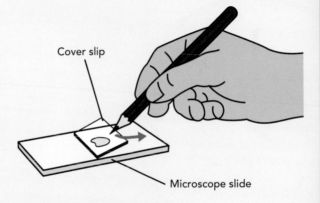

Cover slip

Microscope slide

IMPORTANT: You should never re-use lolly sticks after conducting this experiment, because of the risk of spreading disease.

Specialized cells

Soon after an egg cell begins dividing, the cells start to **differentiate**. This means that some cells become different from others. In an adult, there are about 200 different types of cell. Most of them are specialized for a particular job. Muscle cells can contract (shorten) and relax in order to move the body. Nerve cells have long, thin extensions (nerve fibres) that can carry electrical signals. These signals are used to pass messages to and from the brain.

When cells become specialized for a particular task, they usually lose the ability to divide. Specialized tissues cannot repair themselves. However, some cells, known as **stem cells**, remain unspecialized and keep dividing. Stem cells in the lower layers of the skin, for example, continuously divide in order to replace cells that are lost from the skin surface.

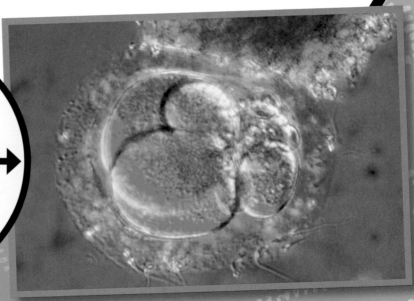

A microscope photo of a very early embryo, when the fertilized egg has divided just a few times. The cells in the centre of the embryo are stem cells that can turn into any kind of cell in the body.

THE SCIENCE YOU LEARN: LIFE PROCESSES

All living things have seven different life processes in common:
1. *Movement*. Animals move from place to place. Plants are rooted to a spot and move much more slowly.
2. *Reproduction*. Animals and plants multiply and produce the next generation of offspring.
3. *Sensitivity*. Animals and plants are sensitive to changes in the environment.
4. *Growth*. Living things grow.
5. *Excretion*. Plants and animals get rid of waste.
6. *Respiration*. This is the process by which cells get energy from food.
7. *Feeding*. Animals and plants need food as a source of energy and growth.

Tissues and organs

Cells in the body are gathered together in large groups to do particular jobs. A group of cells organized in this way is called a tissue. One kind of tissue is called **epithelium**. Epithelium forms a thin membrane that separates different parts of the body, and forms a protective covering. Epithelial cells are not highly specialized, so they can divide. Epithelium can repair itself if it gets damaged. Other important types of tissue are muscles, nerves, and **connective tissue**. Bone, tendons, and ligaments are connective tissues. Blood is also considered to be connective tissue.

An organ is a body part made of two or more different tissues organized together. The heart is an organ. Most of the heart is muscle tissue. The heart muscle tissue contracts and relaxes to pump blood round the body. However, there are also other tissues in the heart. Blood vessels carry oxygen and **nutrients** to the heart muscles. Nerves help to keep the heartbeat strong. Valves made of connective tissue make sure that blood flows the right way through the heart.

Organs can be grouped into systems. The musculoskeletal system includes all the body's bones and skeletal muscles. The heart and blood vessels make up the circulatory system. The lungs and airways make up the respiratory system, while the brain and spinal cord are the main organs of the nervous system.

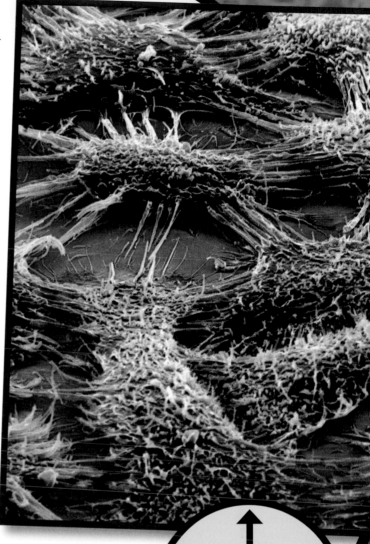

Layers of epithelial cells line the surfaces and cavities of structures throughout our bodies.

Organ	Function
Skin	The skin helps protect the body from disease, reduces water loss, and includes senses of heat, cold, and touch.
Heart	The heart pumps blood around the body.
Brain	The brain is the control centre of the body.
Lungs	The lungs are where oxygen passes into the bloodstream, and carbon dioxide passes out.
Liver	The liver is a chemical factory.
Kidney	The kidney cleans waste products out of the blood.
Stomach	The stomach begins digestion (breakdown) of food.
Small intestine	The small intestine continues the process of digestion and absorbs nutrients (useful substances) from food.
Large intestine	The large intestine absorbs water from the remains of food.
Spleen	The spleen helps protect the body against infection.
Bladder	The bladder stores urine, the waste material produced by the kidneys.

Body system	Function	Main organs
Musculoskeletal system	Supports and moves the body	Bones, muscles
Nervous system	Collects, moves, and processes information	Brain, spinal cord, nerves
Respiratory system	Breathing, exchanging gases between blood and air	Nose, windpipe, lungs
Circulatory system (cardiovascular system)	Moves blood around the body	Heart, blood vessels
Digestive system	Digests (breaks down) and absorbs food	Mouth, oesophagus (food pipe), stomach, small intestine, large intestine
Immune system	Defends the body against disease	Skin, white blood cells, lymph nodes, spleen
Excretory system	Gets rid of waste	Kidneys, bladder

Damaged organs

Some kinds of illness can damage organs so badly that they no longer work properly. The kidneys can be damaged by illnesses such as **diabetes** or high blood pressure. The kidneys filter waste products out of the blood but leave behind useful substances such as proteins, sugars, and other nutrients. If the kidneys are not working, waste products may build up in the blood, or the kidneys may leak, allowing useful substances, such as proteins, to escape in the urine.

Many types of illness can lead to heart damage. The blood vessels that feed the heart muscles (the coronary vessels) can become blocked, so that some of the muscle tissue does not get enough blood. Some muscle tissue may actually die, causing the heart to beat unevenly or stop working altogether.

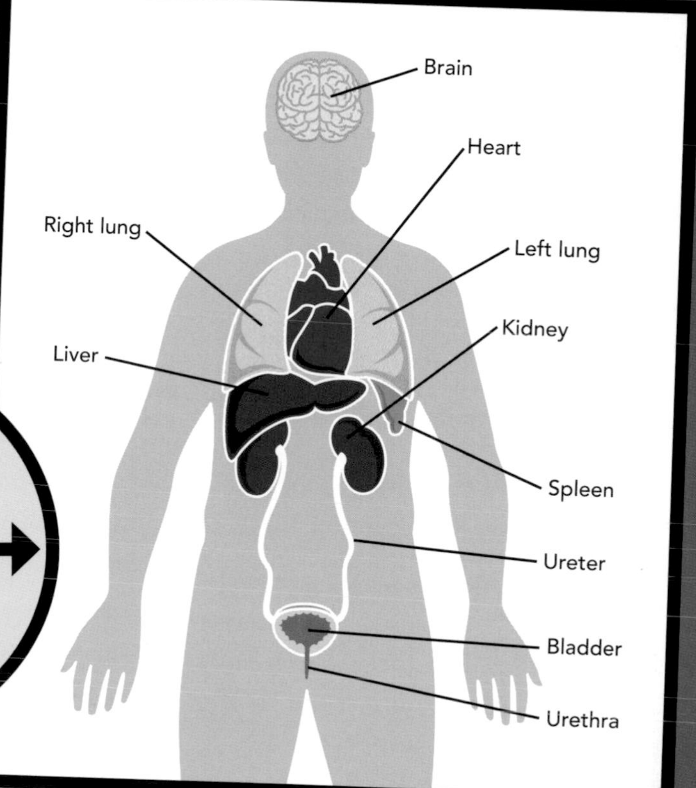

This diagram shows the positions of the major organs in the human body.

Brain

Heart

Right lung

Left lung

Kidney

Liver

Spleen

Ureter

Bladder

Urethra

The lungs can be damaged by emphysema, an illness in which the tiny air sacs break down. They can also be affected by cystic fibrosis, an inherited disorder in which the tubes carrying air into and out of the lungs become blocked with thick, sticky **mucus**. Another important organ is the liver, which is the body's chemical factory and helps control sugar levels in the blood. Hepatitis C, a disease caused by a **virus**, can damage the liver so badly that it hardly works at all. Cancer can also destroy large parts of the liver.

In all these cases, and many others that cause organ damage, doctors will first look for ways to repair the damaged organ, or help it to repair itself. However, if the damage is too severe, an organ transplant may be the only answer.

Repairing organs

Before doctors decide that a patient needs an organ transplant, they will try to repair the organ, or try to help it recover by itself. There are many different ways that an organ can become damaged, and many types of treatment.

Lowering blood pressure

High blood pressure can affect the heart and kidneys. It can damage the blood vessels, and make a **stroke**, kidney failure, heart disease, or a heart attack more likely. Drugs that reduce blood pressure are often used to treat or prevent problems with the heart or kidneys. Different drugs work in different ways. Some are more effective for heart disease, while others work better for the kidneys. Beta-blockers are drugs that block the effects of the **hormone** adrenaline (epinephrine). Adrenalin stimulates the heart to beat faster, so beta-blockers reduce blood pressure by slowing the heart down. This takes some stress off the heart, and helps it to recover.

Angiotensin II blockers are drugs that work better for people with kidney problems. Angiotensin II is a hormone. It causes blood vessels to contract (become narrower), which increases blood pressure. A drug that blocks the action of Angiotensin II helps to decrease blood pressure.

The hormone Angiotensin II also makes the body retain more water. It does this by making the kidneys work harder. An Angiotensin II blocker stops this effect, so the kidneys do not have to work as hard. Resting the kidneys in this way helps them to recover from damage.

Other drugs

Steroids are sometimes used to treat certain types of lung damage. Lung problems can lead to inflammation (swelling), which blocks the airways and makes breathing difficult. Steroids can help to reduce the inflammation.

Sometimes an organ is damaged by infection. If infection is caused by bacteria, treatment with **antibiotics** may clear it and give the organ a chance to heal. However, if infection is caused by a virus it is almost impossible to treat, although doctors and scientists are working to develop new anti-viral drugs against viral infections, such as hepatitis C.

Some organ damage is caused by cancers. Cancers are illnesses in which cells go out of control and divide constantly. One form of treatment is chemotherapy. This involves using very powerful drugs that kill rapidly-dividing cells. Chemotherapy is often effective, but it has unpleasant side-effects such as hair loss and sickness.

Self-repair

Artificial hearts are used to help patients with heart problems while doctors try to find a human donor heart for transplantation. In August 2006, 15-year-old Melissa Mills was admitted to hospital in Edmonton, Canada, with severe heart disease. Doctors were worried that she would not survive long enough for them to find a heart for transplant. They fitted her with an artificial heart.

To everyone's surprise, once the artificial heart had been fitted, Melissa's own heart began to recover its strength. The artificial heart gave Melissa's heart a chance to rest and repair itself.

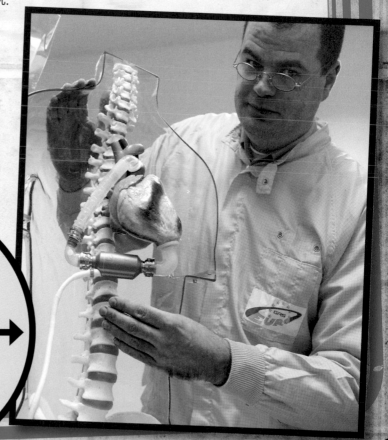

This photo shows a model of the artificial heart, called the Berlin Heart, that was inserted into Melissa Mills. The device was left inside her for 146 days until her own heart was strong enough to function on its own.

Changing lifestyle

Organ damage can be caused by a patient's lifestyle. People who eat a diet rich in fat and do very little exercise are more likely to have heart and blood vessel problems. People who smoke may develop serious lung damage. Those who drink too much alcohol may develop liver damage. In all these cases, changes in the patient's lifestyle are an important part of the treatment. For example, in patients who have narrowed coronary blood vessels, taking more exercise and eating a balanced diet can sometimes cure the patient in the longer term.

Balloons and bypasses

Sometimes, a damaged organ can be fixed or improved by surgery. When a coronary blood vessel is blocked, a technique called **angioplasty** can help. In angioplasty, a small tube called a catheter is inserted into a blood vessel in the groin or in the arm. It is threaded through the blood vessels until it reaches the one that is blocked. Next, a wire is threaded up the catheter and pushed through the blockage.

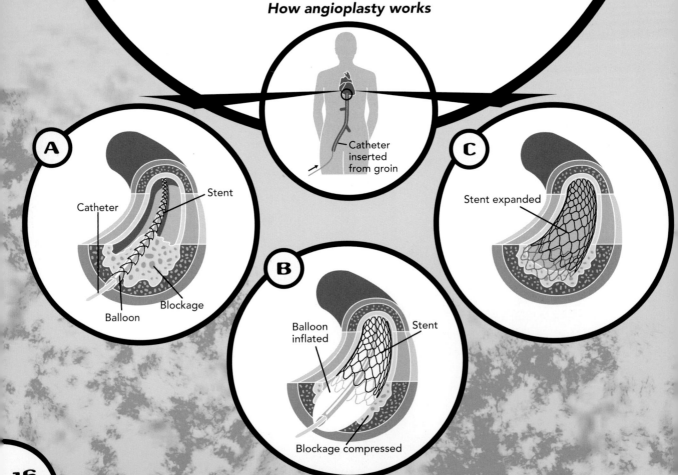

How angioplasty works

Catheter inserted from groin

A — Catheter, Stent, Balloon, Blockage

B — Balloon inflated, Stent, Blockage compressed

C — Stent expanded

Finally, another tube, smaller than the catheter, is pushed up the tube and through the blockage. On the end of this tube there is a tiny balloon. Once the tube is in place, the balloon is inflated. This stretches the walls of the blood vessel and allows blood to flow once more.

Often when an angioplasty is done, a stent is inserted into the blood vessel. This is a small piece of springy mesh tubing. It makes sure the blood vessel does not close up again.

If several of the vessels supplying blood to the heart are narrowed or blocked, an operation called a coronary bypass may help. In this operation, the surgeon takes healthy blood vessels from another part of the body, and uses them to connect vessels that are still working to the areas of the heart that are not getting enough blood.

CASE STUDY

Does angioplasty help?

A medical study on angioplasty shows why it is important to constantly check up on the usefulness and effectivenes of a treatment. The study was carried out on more than 2,000 patients with chronic (long term) angina (heart pain) between 1999 and 2004. Half of the group were given angioplasty, took medicine, ate healthier food, and took more exercise. The other half of the group did not have angioplasty – they just took medicine, ate healthier food, and exercised.

The results were surprising to the doctors and scientists carrying out the test. They found that after five years, the group who did not have an angioplasty were no worse off than the patients who did. They had similar pain relief, and similar numbers had survived without further heart attacks in both groups.

The results of this study are making doctors reconsider how they treat people with chronic angina. However, other studies are needed to make sure that the results of the study are correct and can be trusted. In addition, it does not mean that angioplasty is never useful. For some types of patient angioplasty is a life-saving treatment.

During heart surgery, the heart–lung machine allows the surgeon to stop the patient's heart. The machine takes over the jobs of the heart and the lungs.

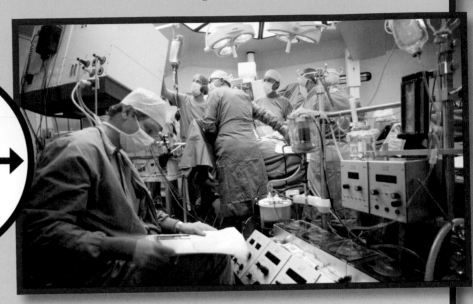

A technician keeps a check on the heart–lung machine during a heart transplant operation.

Normally, blood circulates through the body, then goes to the lungs to collect oxygen and get rid of carbon dioxide. It then comes back to the heart to be pumped around the body once more. In heart surgery, blood coming back from the body goes instead to the heart–lung machine. This consists of a pump and an oxygenator. The pump does the heart's job. It pushes blood first through the oxygenator, and then round the body. The oxygenator does the lungs' job. It adds oxygen and removes carbon dioxide from the blood.

The heart–lung machine can only replace the heart and lungs during an operation. It is large and clumsy, so cannot fit in the body.

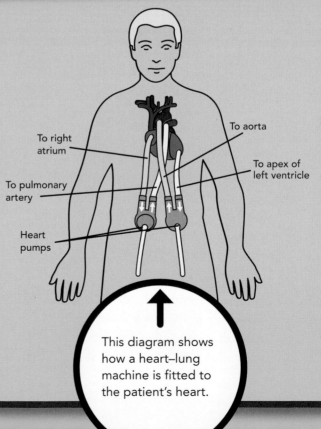

To right atrium

To aorta

To pulmonary artery

To apex of left ventricle

Heart pumps

This diagram shows how a heart–lung machine is fitted to the patient's heart.

Other treatments

One of the most effective treatments for cancer is **radiotherapy**. This involves treating the cancer with high-energy **radiation** such as X-rays. This kind of radiation kills off cells that are rapidly dividing. Cancer cells are most affected by the radiation because they are dividing rapidly, but the radiation can also affect healthy body cells. This can cause side-effects such as hair loss, tiredness, and swellings.

A less extreme kind of radiation can be used to treat some types of cancer. Radiofrequency (RF) ablation is a technique that uses lower energy radiation to heat cancer tissues and kill them. The diagram below shows how the technique works. Doctors use an X-ray or ultrasound scanner to guide a very fine needle into the centre of a **tumour**. Electrical energy is then passed through the needle. This heats up the tissue around the end of the needle, and kills off the cancer cells in the region.

How RF ablation works

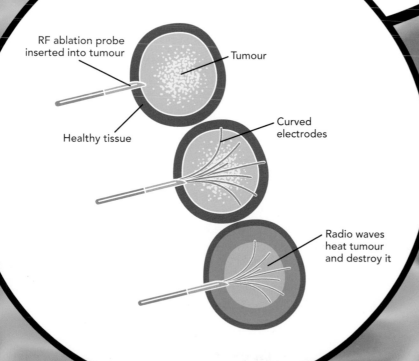

RF ablation probe inserted into tumour

Tumour

Healthy tissue

Curved electrodes

Radio waves heat tumour and destroy it

Organ transplants

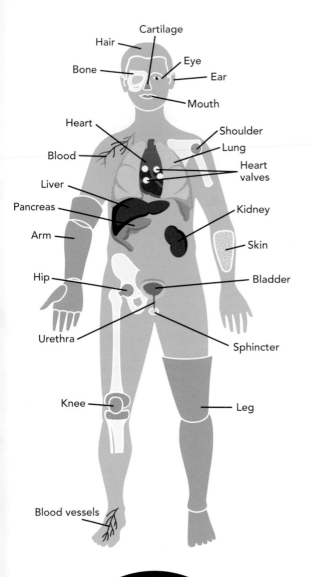

Cartilage
Hair
Bone
Eye
Ear
Mouth
Heart
Shoulder
Lung
Blood
Heart valves
Liver
Pancreas
Kidney
Arm
Skin
Hip
Bladder
Urethra
Sphincter
Knee
Leg
Blood vessels

Nowadays, it is possible to replace or perform transplants on many parts of the body.

Although organs can sometimes be repaired, in other cases damage is so great that the patient has no alternative – he or she must have an organ transplant if they are going to survive.

The earliest organ transplants were kidney transplants. These are still the most common type of transplant operation. Survival rates for kidney transplants are now very good. With other kinds of transplant the chances of success are not as good, but they have improved greatly over the years. Transplants of the heart, liver, lungs, heart and lungs, pancreas (the organ that is damaged in diabetes), and bladder are all possible. Tissues such as the **cornea** of the eye, sections of skin, bone marrow, bone, and heart valves can also be transplanted.

Organ transplant pioneers

The first successful organ transplant was carried out in 1954 by American Dr Joseph E. Murray. Previously, during World War II, Murray had treated wounded soldiers by grafting (transplanting) skin from one person to another. However, he had found that these grafts only worked if the donor and the patient were identical twins. Otherwise, the grafts were rejected.

After the war, Murray experimented with transplanting kidneys in dogs. He found that, as with skin grafts, the transplants were rejected if the dogs were not twins. In 1954, Murray carried out the first successful kidney transplant. The operation was a success because the donor and the patient were identical twins.

In 1956, another American transplant pioneer, E Donnall Thomas, carried out the first bone marrow transplant. The patient had leukaemia (cancer of the white blood cells), and the donor was an identical twin. Thomas began to investigate why transplants often did not work. He found that the problem was caused by a set of proteins on the surface of each person's cells. Only identical twins have the same proteins. From blood tests, Thomas found that some people had similar proteins on their cells. With the help of drugs, transplants between such people could work. Thomas developed methods for matching people whose bone marrow was similar, and in 1969 he was able to perform the first bone marrow transplant between people who were not identical twins.

Other organ transplants were also first made in the 1960s. In 1966 the first successful pancreas transplant was carried out. In 1967, the first ever heart transplant and the first successful liver transplant was carried out.

In a kidney transplant operation, the kidneys are not removed but the new one is placed in a lower position.

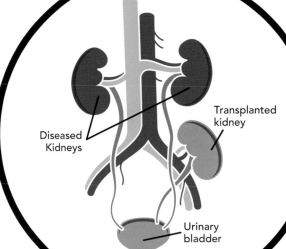

Diseased Kidneys

Transplanted kidney

Urinary bladder

CASE STUDY

The first transplant

The first successful transplantation of tissue was carried out more than 100 years ago, in 1905. An Austrian doctor, Dr Eduard Zirm was the Chief of Medicine at a hospital in Olomouc in Moravia (now part of the Czech Republic). Alois Gloger, a Czech farm worker who was a patient at the hospital, had lost most of the sight in both eyes when the cornea (the eye surface) was scarred by chemical burns. A young boy who was also a patient there had to have an eye removed because something had got inside the eye itself. Dr Zirm took the cornea from the young boy's eye and transplanted it onto Gloger's eyes. For 10 days after the operation, Gloger's eyes were kept sewn shut. However, when the stitches were removed he was able to see again. Three months later he was working, and he was able to see for the rest of his life.

What happens during a heart transplant operation?

Heart transplants normally take about seven hours. The heart is located in the chest, between the two lungs. Once the patient has been **anaesthetized**, the surgeon cuts open the chest, then the breastbone. The ribs are then separated. Next, the surgeon cuts open the **pericardium** – the tough membrane that surrounds the heart. The surgeon then attaches tubes from a heart–lung machine to the blood vessels to and from the heart. The blood vessels are clamped and the blood flows through the heart–lung machine.

The back part of the heart is firmly attached to the chest, so this is not removed. Instead, the front part of the heart is cut away. The back of the donor heart is cut away before the operation starts. The donor heart is sewn in place and the blood vessels attached. The clamps are removed and blood can flow through the new heart. When this happens, the heart should start beating again. In some cases it may just fibrillate (shiver). If this happens, the surgeon gives the heart a short electric shock using a defibrillator. This starts the heart beating properly.

The tubes to the heart–lung machine are removed, and the holes sewn up. The ribcage is closed. The two halves of the breastbone are joined with wire. The chest is finally sewn up with stitches or clips.

A close-up of a heart transplant in progress. The chest cavity has been opened up to expose the heart.

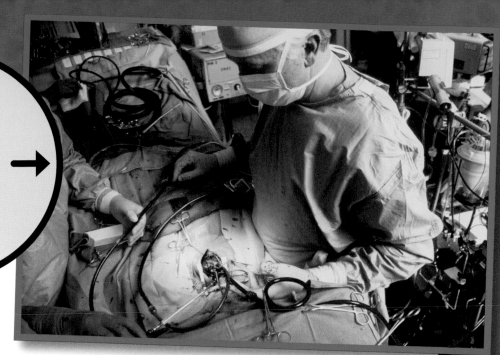

At this stage in the transplant operation, tubes have been inserted to take blood from the body to and from the heart–lung machine. The patient's heart is no longer beating.

Beating-heart transplants

A donor heart is usually transported packed in ice, to keep it fresh. However, cooling an organ can cause damage to the tissue, and it only keeps for about four hours. An American company, TransMedics Inc., has developed a new technique for keeping a donor heart in good condition. Instead of cooling the heart, it is kept at body temperature. The donor's own blood, kept supplied with oxygen and nutrients, is pumped through the heart. Using this technique, the heart can survive longer. This new technique could make it possible to carry out three or four times the current number of heart transplants.

CASE STUDY

Defining death

When surgeons want to remove organs for transplant, they must be certain that the donor is dead. Someone's heart and breathing may stop, but with modern machines it is possible to restart the heart, or keep someone alive on a heart–lung machine. Doctors need to be certain that the brain and brain stem of a patient are dead, and that there is no chance that they may recover, before they will pronounce someone dead.

Becoming a transplant surgeon

Transplant surgery is a difficult and demanding job that involves many years of training. After qualifying as a doctor, a transplant surgeon has to work for at least another eight years, gaining skill as a surgeon but also learning about immunology (the body's defences to disease), **genetics** and other subjects.

A transplant surgeon is very much part of a team. Many other doctors and specialists will be involved in the transplant process. Patients that have had a transplant will continue to see the transplant surgeon and other members of the team for years after the actual operation. The long-term contact with patients can be very rewarding, as the surgeon gets to see a patient's progress towards recovery.

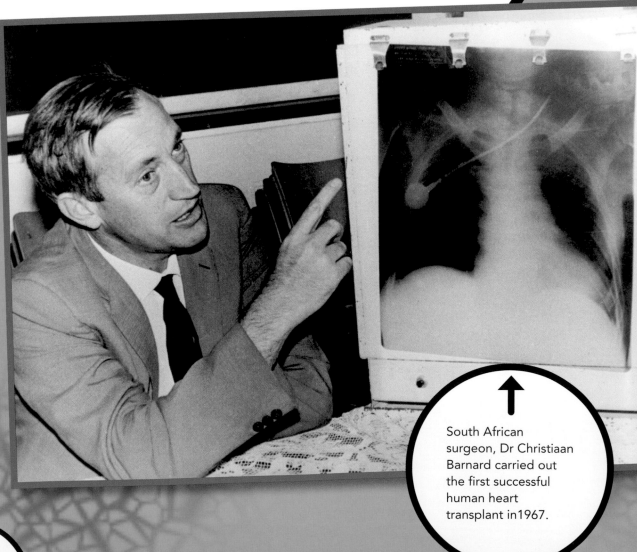

↑ South African surgeon, Dr Christiaan Barnard carried out the first successful human heart transplant in 1967.

CUTTING EDGE: KEEPING THE LIVER GOING

Professor Peter Friend, at the University of Oxford, is a transplant surgeon and researcher. He and his team are researching ways to keep a donor liver working outside the body. They have developed a method for keeping the liver supplied with blood and nutrients, in a similar way to a beating-heart transplant. Using this technique, Friend and his colleagues have kept livers working for 72 hours.

Organ transplant ethics

Some organ transplants are very expensive. In many countries patients have to pay for some or all of their medical care, so poorer people are less likely to get transplants than rich people.

There are many more people needing transplants than there are organs available for transplant. Who should get the organs first? Usually the sickest people are put at the top of the waiting list. However, if someone is given a transplant when they are very weak and ill, they may not survive for long. Is this the best way to decide who gets organs first? Some people need transplants because they have damaged their own organs through smoking or alcohol abuse. Should these people be on the transplant list?

When should the organ be taken? For the best chance of success, organs need to be taken as soon as possible after the donor dies, but when is someone counted as dead? How do the donor's relatives feel about doctors rushing to remove organs from their loved one?

Transplant statistics (USA, 2003)			
Organ	Number receiving transplant	Number on waiting list	Number died while waiting
Heart	2,000	3,500	450
Lung	1,000*	4,000	400
Intestine	100	150	40
Liver	5,000	17,000	2,000
Kidney	14,000	55,000	3,000
Pancreas	450	1,500	30

*One deceased donor can be the source of two lung or liver transplants.
Source: U.S. statistics from Decision: Donation, a schools programme developed by the United States Department of Health.

Transplant problems

The earliest successful transplants used organs donated by identical twins. This is because an organ transplanted from someone who is not a twin causes a problem known as organ rejection. The body's immune system recognizes that the transplant organ is not part of the body. It goes into action and attacks the foreign cells.

"Self" and "not self"

It is important for our bodies to recognize what is "self" and what is "not self". Many living things, such as bacteria, viruses, and other microbes, try to get into our bodies, where they can cause injury and disease.

So how does the body tell the difference between one of its own cells and an invading microbe? It can tell from the cell's signature. Every cell in our body has a collection of proteins on the surface, known as cell recognition proteins. This collection of proteins gives our cells a unique signature, different from the signature of any other living thing (except an identical twin).

Our immune system is designed to defend us against invading microbes and other creatures. The skin is an effective barrier to microbes but if something gets through the skin and into the blood, white blood cells form a second line of defence. There are various types of white blood cell. Some patrol the bloodstream keeping watch for any foreign cells. If they find a cell with the wrong proteins on its surface, they raise the alarm, and other white blood cells rush to the area to destroy the foreign object.

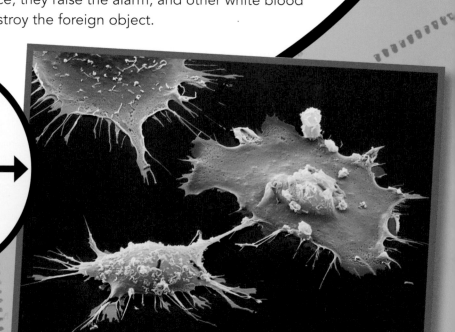

In this micrograph, white blood cells are attacking and engulfing bacteria (small red torpedo shapes). Inside the blood cells the bacteria are destroyed.

If someone has a transplant operation, the organ that is transplanted does not have a matching signature on its cells (unless it comes from an identical twin). The organ is seen as foreign, and even though it is vitally important to the body, the immune system starts trying to destroy it.

Discovering the roots of rejection

Two researchers working separately in different countries discovered the signature proteins on the surface of cells. From 1935 onwards, American biologist George Snell (1903–1996) used mice to investigate the causes of transplant rejection. He found that structures on the surface of the cell determined whether a transplant would be rejected or not. He also showed that these structures were proteins.

French biologist Jean Dausset studied transplant rejection in humans. He found that human cells had surface proteins similar to those of mice. They became known as HLA (human leukocyte antigens). Today, blood tests can show whether the HLA proteins of two people are similar or not. These tests are known as tissue typing.

This computer model shows the shapes of some cell recognition proteins.

Answers to organ rejection

Scientists became aware of the rejection problem early in transplant history. In the 1940s, a group of researchers in Britain, led by the Brazilian-born British scientist, Peter Medawar, showed that mice of one strain rejected skin grafts from another strain of mice. They also showed that this was an immune reaction.

If an organ has a signature similar to that of the body's own cells, the rejection reaction to it is far less than if it has an obviously foreign signature. Doctors look for a donor organ that is a good match to the tissues of the patient. Researchers have found ways to test how well the tissues of different people match – the process is called tissue typing (see box page 27). Doctors look for a donor organ with a tissue type that closely matches that of the patient.

The rejection reaction can be reduced using drugs called immunosuppressants. These are drugs that weaken the immune system. However, they also reduce the body's defences against real threats of infection and disease. Many of the earliest transplant patients died not from the operation, or even from organ rejection, but from infections such as pneumonia. Their bodies could not fight off infections because the immunosuppressant drugs had weakened their immune systems.

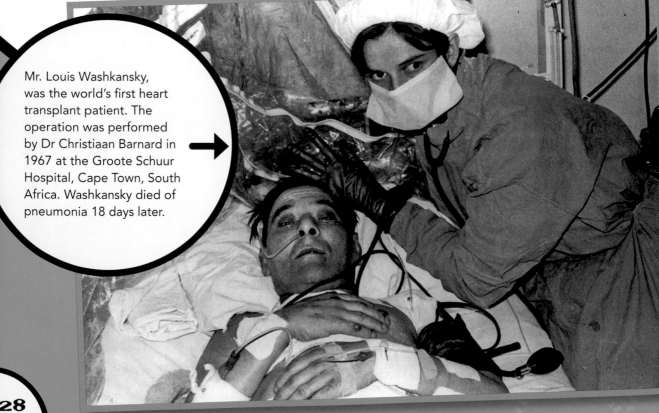

Mr. Louis Washkansky, was the world's first heart transplant patient. The operation was performed by Dr Christiaan Barnard in 1967 at the Groote Schuur Hospital, Cape Town, South Africa. Washkansky died of pneumonia 18 days later.

The percentage of transplant patients in the USA that survive for one year after surgery.										
Organ	1995	1996	1997	1998	1999	2000	2001	2002	2003	2004
Heart	84.6	85.1	85.1	85.7	83.9	85.9	85.6	87.1	88.2	88.2
Lung	75.7	71.1	76.0	76.2	76.2	77.2	77.9	81.7	84.5	85.8
Intestine	68.0	68.0	57.8	67.5	59.9	75.1	72.1	76.8	81.1	79.7
Heart–lung	80.0	63.5	60.0	57.3	55.7	63.5	74.6	61.9	55.3	75.7
Liver deceased donor	83.6	83.5	85.4	85.5	84.8	86.4	85.7	86.9	86.5	87.3
Liver living donor	79.8	88.9	85.9	79.4	81.4	86.8	88.0	85.3	90.8	92.3
Kidney deceased donor	94.2	94.7	94.2	95.1	94.5	94.4	95.0	95.2	95.3	95.6
Kidney living donor	97.0	97.8	97.4	97.9	97.9	97.8	97.8	98.0	98.5	98.3
Pancreas	91.5	–	91.9	98.2	96.6	–	97.0	97.4	93.7	96.0

[Source: The U.S. Organ Procurement and Transplantation Network and the Scientific Registry of Transplant Recipients. 2004 figures.]

CUTTING EDGE: BETTER REJECTION PROTECTION

Immunosuppressive drugs are effective, but they cause side effects. Some drugs raise blood pressure, which increases the risk of a heart attack. Others cause gradual damage to the kidneys, and some cause **anaemia** (fewer red blood cells in the blood). However, new research at the drug company Pfizer has led to the discovery of an experimental drug that may avoid these side effects.

Current immunosuppressants affect all cells, which is why they have such bad side effects. The new drug, however, targets a protein in the body called JAK-3. This protein is only active in the cells of the immune system, so the drug only affects the immune system. JAK-3 is part of a signalling system that sends out distress signals to the white blood cells when a part of the body is infected. The idea is that by targeting JAK-3, the distress signals are not sent out and white blood cells will not attack the new organ.

Artificial body parts

One solution to the problem of rejection could be to make an artificial replacement for the patient's failing organ. Scientists and engineers have worked together to build replacements for many body parts, from false teeth to electrically-operated limbs. Making artificial replacements for organs such as the heart and the kidney has proved more difficult.

False teeth and peg legs

The earliest types of artificial body parts were prostheses. These are replacements for body parts that have had to be removed such as a hand or foot. False teeth are also prostheses.

 SCIENCE YOU LEARN: LIMBS ARE LEVERS

Our arms and legs are very well-designed machines. They are levers. Each of the joints is the fulcrum (pivot point) of the lever. The elbow joint is the fulcrum for the lower part of the arm. When you pick up a drink, the drink in your hand is the load. When you bend your arm the biceps muscle contracts, and this supplies the effort needed to lift the load. The effort is greater than the load, because it is closer to the fulcrum than the load.

Engineers designing artificial limbs need to calculate the effort needed to lift common loads, so that the motors in the limbs are powerful enough.

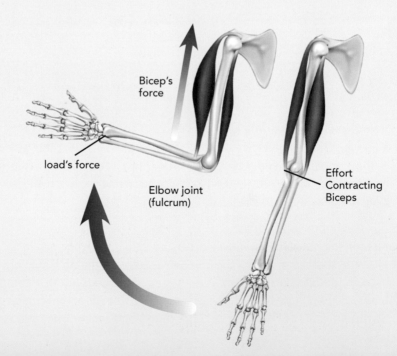

Bicep's force

load's force

Elbow joint (fulcrum)

Effort Contracting Biceps

Early limb replacements were simple objects such as a wooden leg, or a hook in place of a hand. Artificial limbs of this kind have been around for thousands of years. An Egyptian mummy more than 2,500 years old has been found with artificial copper toes. In 1504, a replacement for the lower arm was made for the German soldier Götz von Berlichingen (1480–1562). It was made of iron, and the hand could be manually opened and closed.

Modern artificial limbs can be moved using electric motors. In a myoelectric limb, the patient controls the movement of the limb by contracting muscles in the upper arm or leg. The artificial limb has **electrodes** that pick up electrical signals in muscles. The electrodes are connected to the electric motors in the artificial limb, and turn the motors on and off according to the muscle signals.

Artificial joints

Joints can be damaged by several kinds of illness, but are most commonly affected by arthritis. Arthritis is an illness caused by inflammation (swelling) or other damage to joints. This results in pain and difficulty in moving the joint. In some types of arthritis, the joint becomes damaged over time. In such cases, the best treatment may be to replace one or both parts of the joint with artificial parts.

Artificial legs do not always have to work like real legs. South African athlete Oscar Pistorius is one of many **amputee** runners who use carbon-fibre artificial legs for racing. The legs are springy, and help the runner to power around the athletics track. For running, they are more efficient than our own legs.

Knees and hips

Knees and hips are the most common joint replacements. In both cases, the joint surfaces and some bone are first removed. New ends are fitted to both bones. In the knee joint, the end of the thigh bone (the femur) is rounded, while the end of the shin bone (the tibia) is fairly flat. Both new pieces are made of metal but a plastic piece is fitted over the tibia surface.

The artificial bone ends have attachments that insert into the remaining bone. Sometimes the artificial parts are cemented in place, but in other cases no cement is used, and the bone grows around the implant to hold it still.

The joint surfaces are **lubricated** with an oily liquid called synovial fluid. →

Synovial membrane

Articular cartilage

Joint cavity filled with synovial fluid

Fibrous joint capsule

Ligaments

THE SCIENCE YOU LEARN: JOINTS AND JOINT DAMAGE

Wherever two different bones come together in the body, there is a joint. Joints allow bones to move in relation to each other. Shoulder, wrist, and hip joints allow a large range of movement in several directions. The elbow and knee have a more limited range, and individual joints in the spine can only move a small amount. Skull joints are designed to hold bones firmly together rather than to allow movement. However, even these joints have some flexibility.

In joints that move a lot, such as the shoulder, hip, elbow, and knee, there is a layer of

cartilage over the bone ends, where the joint surfaces rub against each other. Cartilage is smoother than bone and slightly springy, so it cushions the joint and makes a better surface for the moving parts. In some kinds of arthritis, the cartilage in the joint begins to wear abnormally and the joint surfaces no longer move smoothly against each other. The bones of the joints can also grow spurs (lumps), which make joint movement even more difficult and painful.

Kidney machines

A machine that could remove waste substances from the blood was first used to treat a patient with kidney failure in 1943. The machine used a process called dialysis. The diagram below shows how dialysis works. Blood flows through a tube made of cellophane. Outside the tube is a liquid flowing the other way. This liquid contains sugars and other nutrients at similar concentrations to those found in blood. However, unlike blood, this liquid contains no waste substances. The cellophane is semi-permeable – it allows small molecules to pass through it. Because there are no waste substances outside the tube, waste flows out of the tube and is carried away.

Dialysis machines are large and bulky – too big to be placed in the body. A patient with kidney failure can be kept alive indefinitely using a dialysis machine, but it involves spending hours hooked up to the machine several times a week.

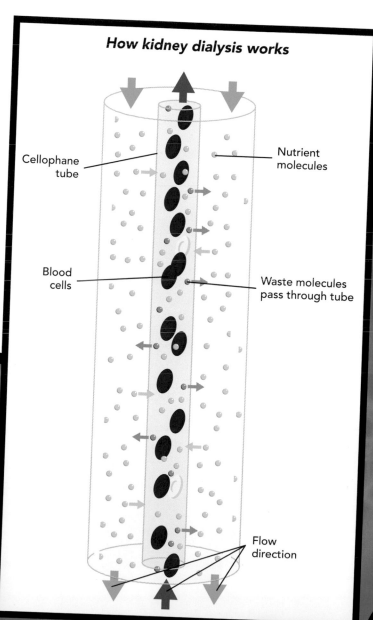

How kidney dialysis works

Cellophane tube

Nutrient molecules

Blood cells

Waste molecules pass through tube

Flow direction

33

Artificial hearts

Research into using artificial hearts began in Russia in the 1930s. Two kinds of device were tested. One was a total artificial heart, which replaced the heart completely. The other was something known as a ventricular assist device (VAD). This is fitted in one of the **ventricles** of the heart. It helps a failing heart to pump blood round the body.

THE SCIENCE YOU LEARN: ANATOMY OF THE HEART

The heart has four chambers: two atria, where blood collects as it comes into the heart, and two ventricles, which pump the blood out from the heart. The left ventricle is largest, and pumps blood around the body. The smaller right ventricle pumps blood to the lungs.

VADs assist the ventricles of the heart by adding to their pumping power. In a left ventricle assist device (LVAD), blood coming out of the ventricle goes into the VAD, then out through a tube that connects to the aorta (main artery carrying blood to the body).

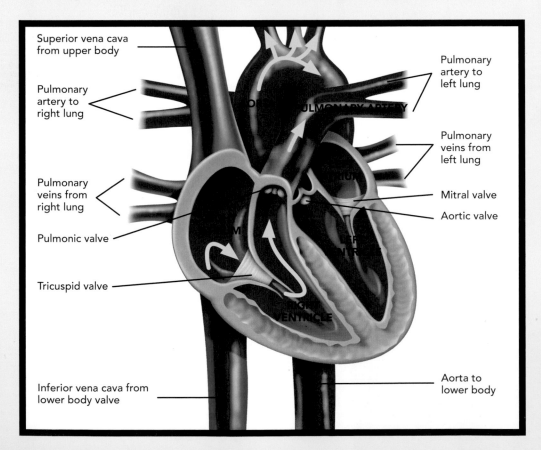

Superior vena cava from upper body

Pulmonary artery to right lung

Pulmonary veins from right lung

Pulmonic valve

Tricuspid valve

Inferior vena cava from lower body valve

Pulmonary artery to left lung

Pulmonary veins from left lung

Mitral valve

Aortic valve

Aorta to lower body

The first total artificial heart transplant was carried out in 1967 in Houston, Texas, USA. The patient was kept alive for 64 hours using the artificial heart, before it was replaced by a heart from a donor. Unfortunately, the patient died from a lung infection. An improved artificial heart, the *Jarvik-7*, was developed in the 1970s by American physician Robert Jarvik (see box page 36). The first patient to receive the *Jarvik-7* heart survived for 112 days, but it soon became clear that the heart was not a reliable replacement for a natural heart. However, it is used to keep patients alive for a limited time while they wait for a heart transplant.

Assist devices

Ventricular assist devices (VADs) have proved more useful than complete artificial hearts. A VAD is a small pump powered either by electricity or by compressed air. It helps a weak or damaged heart by adding to its pumping power. Some larger VADs are used outside the body, while others are implanted. The battery pack or other power source is always outside the body, so that the batteries can be changed regularly.

Usually a VAD is used to assist the left ventricle as this is the one that pumps blood around the body.

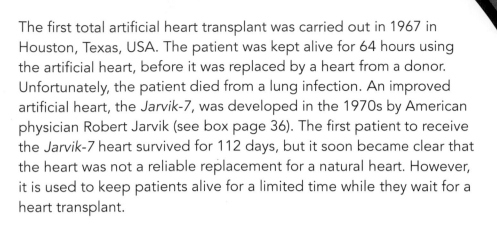

Aorta

Left ventricle

LVAD

Robert Jarvik: expert heart-maker

The first widely-used artificial heart was named the Jarvik-7 after Dr Robert Jarvik. It was first used as a heart replacement in the 1970s. However, this kind of heart was bulky and required a large power pack and control system outside the heart.

In 1987 Dr Jarvik set up his own company. Instead of producing a full artificial heart, they developed a small LVAD called the Jarvik 2000. Early VADs used a pump that pulsed like the heart itself, but the Jarvik 2000 is one of a new generation of much smaller, simpler VADs. The pump in these new VADs is a rotating **turbine**.

Tissue engineering

Until recently, artificial body parts were made from metal, plastic, or other materials. However, recent research has focused on growing artificial body parts rather than making them. This field of research is known as tissue engineering.

Scientists have been growing cells in the laboratory for many years. With the right mixture of nutrients, and in the right conditions, **cell cultures** can be kept and grown in the laboratory. In tissue engineering, cells are grown in combination with other materials, or into particular shapes, in order to create artificial tissues and organs.

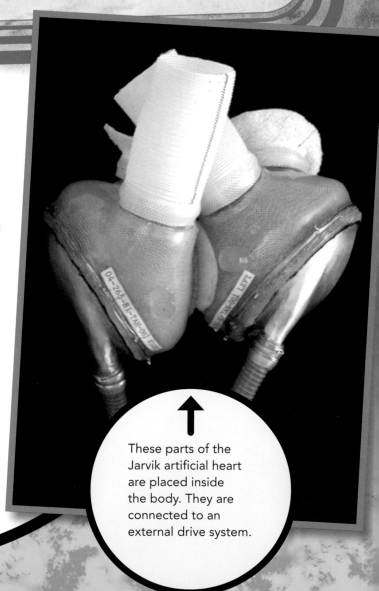

These parts of the Jarvik artificial heart are placed inside the body. They are connected to an external drive system.

One area of research involves trying to make artificial skin. When people suffer bad burns, surgeons help the burns to heal by grafting skin from other parts of the body onto the burns. However, when someone has extensive burns, it is hard to find enough places to take skin from. Experiments with growing artificial skin may solve this problem. The artificial skin is a mixture of cells and a tough, fibrous material called fibrin, which naturally forms during the healing of wounds. Initial experiments with this combination have been very successful.

CUTTING EDGE: GROWING NEW ORGANS

The first artificial organs to be grown in a laboratory were bladders. These were transplanted into seven patients with bladder problems in April 2006. A team of scientists at Wake Forest University in North Carolina, USA, grew the bladders from small samples of cells from the patients' own bladders. The samples were first grown in cell culture to increase their numbers. The cells were then added to a bladder-shaped scaffolding made from a protein called collagen.

A bladder is little more than a simple bag, so this is only a small step towards real tissue engineering. However, other scientists are working on developing artificial kidneys and even livers using a similar technique.

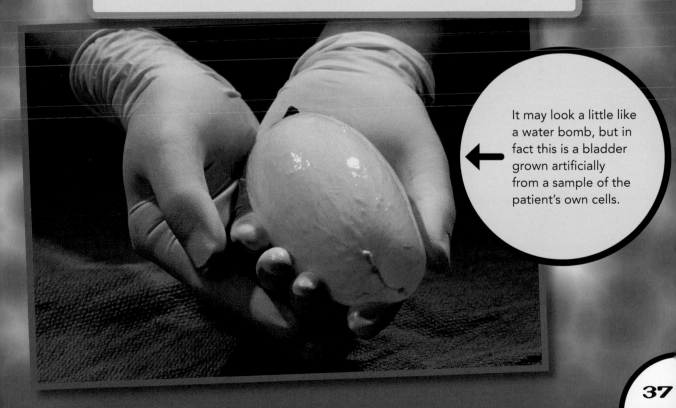

It may look a little like a water bomb, but in fact this is a bladder grown artificially from a sample of the patient's own cells.

Stem cells

The most exciting new developments in the field of organ transplants involve stem cells. Research into stem cells offers the prospect of repairing organs that cannot repair themselves, or growing tailor-made organs to replace parts that have become damaged.

What are stem cells?

Cells divide to allow the body to grow and repair itself. When cells become specialized to do a particular job, they often lose this ability to divide. Stem cells do not become specialized, and so keep the ability to divide. In fact, they can keep dividing, again and again, almost indefinitely. If conditions are right, a small group of stem cells can produce millions of new cells.

THE SCIENCE YOU LEARN: CELL DIVISION

The process of cell division is called **mitosis**. The main part of the process happens in the period before the cell starts to divide. The cell makes a copy of all the DNA (genetic material) in the nucleus of the cell. Once this has been done, the DNA coils itself up into long structures called chromosomes. The membrane around the nucleus dissolves, and the chromosomes separate into two identical sets, one at each side of the cell. Once this has happened, the cell itself divides in two, and a new nuclear membrane forms around each set of chromosomes.

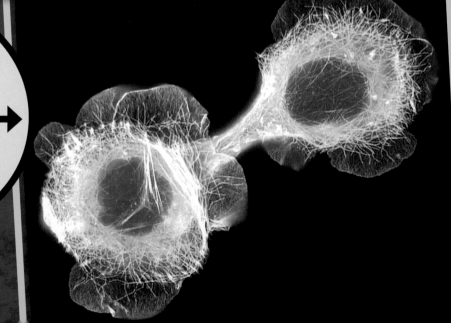

This picture shows a cell in the final stages of dividing into two. The nucleus (purple) has already divided, and the body of the cell is almost completely separated.

This is a micrograph of a cluster of human embryonic stem cells. These cells can be used for scientific research but it is a controversial issue.

As well as being able to divide, stem cells can also differentiate into other types of cell. In adults, stem cells in particular tissues turn into the specialized cells found in that kind of tissue. For example, there are many stem cells in bone marrow, where new blood cells are formed. These stem cells can differentiate to become red blood cells or white blood cells. They can also form cell fragments called platelets, which are important for blood clotting.

A human being begins life as a single cell, and early on in the development of an **embryo**, the cells begin to differentiate. At this stage, the embryo is a hollow ball of cells. Inside this hollow ball, at one end, is a group of about 30 stem cells. These are known as embryonic stem cells. Embryonic stem cells are different from those in an adult because they are far more versatile (changeable). An embryonic stem cell can differentiate into almost any other type of cell.

What stem cells do

In an adult, stem cells are an essential part of the body's repair mechanism. Most organs and tissues contain small groups of stem cells. They have been found in the brain, blood vessels, muscles, skin, and liver. However, not all organs and tissues have the same ability to repair themselves.

Bone marrow contains many stem cells because some blood cells wear out very quickly. Red blood cells last a few months, but some types of white blood cell last only a few hours. The bone marrow has to produce around 10,000 billion new cells every day just to replace those that naturally wear out. A second set of stem cells in the bone marrow produces new bone and cartilage cells.

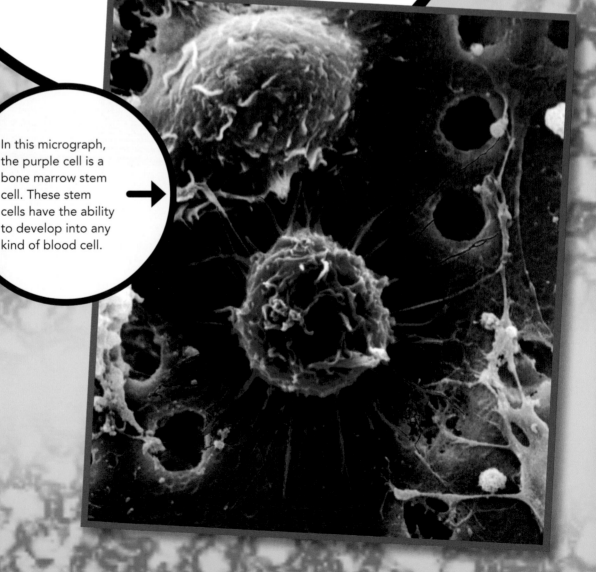

In this micrograph, the purple cell is a bone marrow stem cell. These stem cells have the ability to develop into any kind of blood cell.

In other organs and tissues, there are far fewer stem cells, and they have less ability to repair and renew tissue. In most tissues, the stem cells are found in a specific area, and they are inactive most of the time. They only become active if disease or injury causes damage to the tissue.

In contrast, embryonic stem cells are very active. The 30 cells in the early embryo divide and produce all the different cells, tissues, and organs that make up a human. After 9 months in the womb, the 30 cells have become billions, and the ball of cells is a newborn baby.

CUTTING EDGE: THE STEM CELL DEBATE

There is a continuing debate about how ethical it is to do research using embryonic stem cells. Some people think that human embryos should not be used for scientific research. They argue that embryos are human beings, no matter how young they are, and that destroying them to harvest stem cells is taking human life.

There are strict regulations about how stem cells can be used for research. The regulations vary between countries. In the United Kingdom, anyone wishing to carry out embryonic stem cell research has to get approval from a panel of experts known as the Human Fertilisation and Embryology Authority. In the United States, the government will not fund research projects using embryonic stem cells. This means that very little of this kind of research is carried out.

Stem cells from embryos

For many years, stem cells from mouse embryos have been grown in laboratories and used for research. In 1998, the first stem cells were isolated from a human embryo. Human embryonic stem cells come from eggs donated by women undergoing fertility treatment. Each egg is fertilized in the laboratory, and grown until it forms a ball of cells. Once a ball of cells has been checked, it can be put into the mother's womb where it develops like any other baby. The remaining embryos can be used for stem cell research.

Stem cell research

Scientists have used the techniques learned with mouse cells to grow human embryonic stem cells in the laboratory. As long as the cells are kept under certain conditions, they will keep growing and dividing as non-specialized stem cells. However, if groups of cells are allowed to clump together, they begin to change and differentiate into different cell types. By allowing clumping and carefully controlling the conditions, scientists have learned how to choose which types of cell the stem cells become. So far, they have managed to make the stem cells turn into nerve cells and muscle cells, amongst others. In recent research, scientists have created **insulin**-producing cells from embryonic stem cells. These cells could be used to treat diabetes.

If stem cells can be grown in large numbers, and changed into specialized tissue such as nerve and muscle, then eventually it could be possible to grow replacement tissues and organs. In the shorter term, stem cells could be used to stimulate damaged organs to produce new tissue. Experiments in mice have shown that treating a damaged heart with stem cells stimulates the damaged heart muscles to regrow.

IN THE NEWS:
PROBLEMS WITH EMBRYONIC STEM CELLS

There are two problems with using embryonic stem cells in this way. First, many people think it is **unethical** to experiment with human embryos. Some cultures and religious traditions oppose the use of human life as a means to some other end, even if the purpose is a good one. In addition, the governments of certain countries will not fund research using embryonic stem cells.

The second problem is that embryonic stem cells from a donor will not have the same genetic make-up as the patient. Organs and tissues using embryonic stem cells would have the same problem of rejection as normal transplants.

Adult stem cell research

Until recently, adult stem cell research has had less success than embryonic stem cell research. There are two main reasons for this. First, adult stem cells can only differentiate into a limited number of different specialized cells. The second reason is also important. To date, scientists have not been able to grow adult stem cells for long periods, and increase their numbers, in the way they can with embryonic stem cells.

Each of these pots contains stem cells being grown in the laboratory. By adding chemicals to the liquid they grow in, it is possible to stimulate the cells to differentiate into particular cell types.

Stimulating changes

Recent research has shown that adult stem cells may be far more useful than originally thought. Experiments have demonstrated that some types of stem cell can be stimulated to change into other types of cell besides the ones that they form in the body. Bone marrow stem cells, for example, have been differentiated into nerve cells, muscle cells, heart muscle cells, and liver cells. Stem cells from the brain have been turned into blood cells and muscle cells.

Adult stem cells also have the huge advantage over embryonic stem cells that they can be taken from the patient's own body, and so any tissues or organs grown from them will be genetically identical to the patient.

Using stem cells

Scientists are still a long way from growing new organs and tissues from either embryonic stem cells or adult stem cells. However, stem cells are already being tested in the treatment of some diseases. For example, adult stem cells (from a patient's bone marrow) have been used to try and treat some types of heart disease by stimulating the heart to repair itself. The results of such experiments are not yet clear.

At present, scientists are able to do far more with embryonic stem cells than with adult stem cells. Cutting edge developments do suggest that in the near future we may be able to turn adult cells into highly flexible "embryonic" stem cells. A great deal more research will be needed before stem cells can solve the problems of transplant treatments, but they do hold a very bright hope for the future.

CUTTING EDGE: STEM CELLS FROM SKIN

In November 2007, two separate groups of scientists managed to reprogramme human skin cells to make them almost exactly like embryonic stem cells. Groups of scientists in Japan and the United States took skin cells from a human donor, and used specially modified viruses to turn on four inactive **genes** in the cells. Once these **dormant** genes had been activated, the cells behaved like embryonic stem cells (see page 44). They could be grown in the laboratory, and converted into all kinds of different specialized cells, including muscles, nerves, and gut cells.

Skin cell is removed, in this case, from the face of a 36-year-old woman.

The modified viruses, designed to activate four particular genes, are injected into the skin cell.

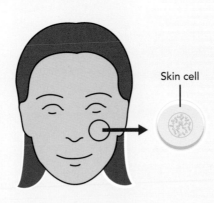

As the dormant genes become activated by the viruses, they make the skin cell behave almost like an embryonic stem cell.

Once the cell is reprogrammed, it can be made to generate any type of tissue.

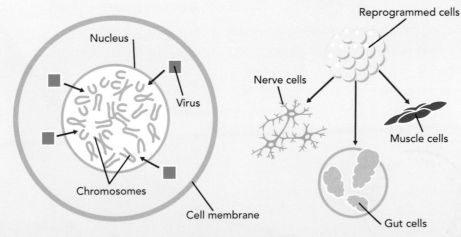

Conclusion

Transplant medicine has developed a tremendous amount since the early transplants were made in the 1950s. Scientists have also learned a great deal about the body. They have learned more about how the organs work, about the immune system, about genetics, and about stem cells. There is no immediate answer to the shortage of organ donors, but despite this problem, transplant surgery has been a success. The total numbers of transplants are rising, more organs can be transplanted than were possible in the past, and a patient's chance of surviving for years after the transplant are far higher than in earlier transplants.

Future prospects

In conventional surgery, new methods for keeping donated organs alive and fresh promise to make it possible to keep donor organs for longer. This could greatly increase the numbers of organs available for transplant. New, better-targeted drugs for preventing organ rejection should give transplant patients a better chance of recovering and living a normal life after their transplant.

Developments in the field of artificial organs are also promising. Although artificial hearts cannot completely replace a real heart, new heart-assist devices could be used as permanent support devices for damaged or weakened hearts. For other organs, tissue engineering looks to be the most promising way of developing artificial replacements.

In the longer term, stem cells offer the greatest hope for the future. For some years, stem cell research has moved more slowly than expected, but recent breakthroughs offer real evidence that the research is progressing and working. It seems almost certain that in the not too distant future, it will be possible to repair seriously damaged organs, and even to replace damaged organs and tissues, using stem cells taken from the patient's own body. An idea that might have been dismissed as science fiction 10 years ago is now a real possibility.

The World Transplant Games

Yearly proof that transplant surgery is worthwhile can be seen at The World Transplant Games. People who have had organ transplants compete against each other in sporting events for the glory of a World Transplant Games gold medal. The Games have been held every year since 1978. Summer Games are held once every other year, and winter Games are held in the years in-between. In 2007, more than 1,500 competitors from 68 countries took part in the summer Games in Bangkok, Thailand. Top of the medal table was Great Britain, with 277 medals. Second and third places went to Australia, with 87 medals, and the United States, with 81 medals.

Australian Seona Rough has had a kidney transplant. In the 2007 World Transplant Games she won a gold medal in the women's shot put.

Facts and figures

Biographies

John Heysham Gibbon (1903–1973) was born in Philadelphia, USA, where he trained to be a surgeon. In 1931 one of his young patients died while he was performing a lung operation on her. Gibbon thought that if he had been able to keep her blood supplied with oxygen while he was operating, she would have lived. This was when he began to work on the idea of a heart–lung machine. Progress was slow until 1946, when he teamed up with Thomas D. Watson, the head of the company IBM. Watson sent Gibbon a team of five engineers to help sort out the problems with his machine. After tests on cats and dogs, the heart–lung machine was successfully used on a young patient with heart problems in 1953.

Edward Donnall Thomas (born 1920) was born and raised in Texas, USA. He trained at Harvard Medical School before going into medical research. For a time he worked at the same Boston hospital as Joseph E. Murray, and he helped care for the first kidney transplant patient. While he was a professor at Columbia University he began research on bone marrow transplants. He and his team worked at first on dogs, then in 1956 he carried out a successful bone marrow transplant between two identical twins. However, it took another 14 years, during which time tissue typing and anti-rejection drugs were developed, before he was able to successfully transplant bone marrow from a donor who was not a twin. He shared the 1990 Nobel Prize for Medicine with Joseph E. Murray.

Joseph E. Murray (born 1919), was born in Milford, USA, and he trained as a doctor at Harvard Medical School. During World War II he worked in an Army hospital, and he noticed how skin grafts given to burn victims were gradually rejected. He found that only a graft from an identical twin was not rejected. After the war, working in Boston, he investigated whether the same was true of internal organs. After some work on dogs, in 1954 he carried out a successful kidney transplant between identical twins. In the early 1960s the first anti-rejection drugs were developed. In 1962 Murray used these drugs to help carry out the first successful kidney transplant between unrelated people. He shared the 1990 Nobel Prize for Medicine with E. Donnall Thomas for his work.

Sir Peter Medawar (1915–1987) was born in Rio de Janeiro, Brazil. His mother was English and his father was Lebanese. He went to England in 1932 to study Zoology at Oxford University, and stayed on there to do research. Like Joseph E. Murray, he became interested in the rejection of skin grafts while treating burn victims during World War II. In experiments with mice carried out after the war he found that if he injected cells from one mouse into another mouse before it was born, the injected mouse did not reject skin grafts from the first mouse. In 1960 Medawar shared the Nobel Prize With Sir MacFarlane Burnet for this and other research into rejection of foreign tissue.

Jean Dausset (born 1916) was born in Toulouse, France. He moved to Paris aged 11, and later studied medicine there. His studies were interrupted by World War II, during which he worked in a hospital in North Africa. This was where he first became interested in blood and blood transfusions. In his research after the war, he noticed that people who had repeated transfusions had very low numbers of leucocytes (white blood cells). He found that the "foreign" leucocytes in the transfusions were being killed off by **antibodies** in the blood. Further experiments showed that special proteins on the leucocytes, called HLA proteins, were causing the antibody attack. The HLA proteins were a key part of how the body distinguishes between "self" and "not self". In 1980 Dausset shared the Noble Prize for Medicine with George D. Snell and Baruj Benacerraf for this work.

Number of transplants per year in the United States, 1988–2005								
	1988	1990	1995	2000	2001	2003	2004	2005
Heart	1,676	2,107	2,363	2,198	2,202	2,056	2,016	2,127
Heart/Lung	74	52	69	48	27	29	39	33
Intestine	—	5	46	82	111	116	152	178
Kidney	8,873	9,416	11,081	13,612	14,263	15,134	15,999	16,477
Kidney/Pancreas	171	459	919	915	891	870	880	903
Liver	1,713	2,690	3,934	4,995	5,185	5,669	6,167	6,444
Lung	33	203	872	959	1,058	1,085	1,173	1,408
Pancreas	78	69	109	472	438	502	603	541
Total: All organs	**12,618**	**15,001**	**19,393**	**23,248**	**24,208**	**25,461**	**27,029**	**28,111**

Source: United States National Organ Procurement and Transplantation Network

Transplant timeline

1504 A replacement lower arm made for the German soldier Götz von Berlichingen. It was made of iron, and the hand could be opened and closed.

1901– Discovery of ABO blood groups.

1903 Viennese physician Karl Landsteiner points out that adverse reactions that occur when humans receive blood from animals may also occur when humans receive blood from other humans. His suggestions receive little attention until 1909, when he classifies human blood into the A, B, AB, and O groups and shows that catastrophic reactions can occur when a person receives blood from a different group. Compatibility is later found to be not only a requirement for transfusion but for transplantation. In 1930, Landsteiner wins the Nobel Prize in Medicine for his discovery of human blood groups.

1906 First successful cornea transplant by Dr. Eduard Zirm. Few other surgeons match Zirm's success until after World War II, when very fine needles and finer silk become available.

1933 First kidney transplant. Russian Dr Yuriy Yurievich Voronoy transplants a kidney into a 26-year-old woman whose own kidneys have been poisoned. She lives for only 4 days after the operation.

1944 Sir Peter Medawar first discovers the immune system is to blame for the failure of all previous organ transplant experiments.

1953 First operation using a heart–lung machine. The operation was performed by US doctor John Heysham Gibbon, who invented the machine. He successfully operated on 18-year-old Cecelia Bayolek.

1954 Dr Joseph E. Murray performs the first successful kidney transplant in Boston, USA, transplanting Ronald Herrick's kidney into his twin brother Richard. Richard marries his nurse and lives another eight years.

1955 First heart valve transplant. Dr Gordon Murray of Toronto, Canada, uses a heart valve from a car accident victim to perform the world's first heart valve transplant. The transplanted valve worked well for over eight years.

1956 First bone marrow transplant. American Dr Edward Donnall Thomas performs a bone marrow transplant between identical twins, one of whom had leukaemia.

1962 First anti-rejection drug. Americans Gertrude B. Elion and George H. Hitchings develop the anti-rejection drug Imuran, which blocks the body's rejection of foreign tissues. They receive a Nobel Prize in 1988 for their discoveries.

1962 First kidney transplant using a kidney from a dead donor. New tissue typing techniques and anti-rejection drugs are used for the first time in a human kidney transplant in Boston, USA.

1966 First pancreas transplant. Dr Richard C. Lillehei and Dr William D. Kelly of the University of Minnesota, in the United States, transplant a pancreas into a 28-year-old woman. She dies three months later from a lung disease.

1967 First heart transplant. South African surgeon Dr Christiaan Barnard performs the first successful human heart transplant. The patient lives for 18 days before dying of pneumonia.

1967 First successful liver transplant. American Dr Thomas E. Starzl performs the first successful liver transplant in Colorado, USA.

1969 First artificial heart transplant. Dr Denton A. Cooley, in Texas, USA, implants the first total artificial heart (the Liotta Total Artificial Heart) into a 47-year-old patient, Haskell Karp. The artificial heart is used as a temporary measure until Karp receives a donor heart 64 hours later.

1970 First successful bone marrow transplant. Dr Edward Donnell Thomas, working in Seattle, USA, performs the first successful bone marrow transplant between people who were not twins.

1973 A team of doctors in New York City performs the first bone marrow transplant using a donor not related to the patient. After seven transplants, their blood function becomes normal.

1977 Anti-rejection drug cyclosporin discovered. The drug is discovered by a team led by Dr Jean Borel in Basel, Switzerland. Cyclosporin revolutionizes organ transplantation because it allows the patient to tolerate the grafted organ but prevents routine infections.

1981 First successful heart–lung transplant. Dr Bruce Reitz of Stanford University in California, USA, performs the first successful heart–double lung transplant on 45-year-old Mary D. Golke. Golke died in 1986.

1982 First permanent heart transplant. In Utah, USA, Dr William DeVries implants a *Jarvik-7* heart into retired dentist Barney Clark. Mr Clark lives 112 days.

1983 First successful single lung transplant. Dr Joel Cooper of Toronto General Hospital in Canada performs a single lung transplant on 58-year-old Tom Hall. Hall lives for more than six years before dying of kidney failure.

1986 First successful double lung transplant. Dr Joel Cooper performs a double lung transplant on Ann Harrison. Harrison lives until 2001, when she dies of a brain problem.

1998 Two research groups in the United States independently announce that they have produced stem cell lines from human embryonic tissue.

2000 The first use of the *Jarvik-2000*, a tiny device implanted into the heart that may help to reduce the need for heart transplants. Human embryonic stem cells cultured in the laboratory for the first time.

2007 Two teams of researchers, led by Dr Shinya Yamanaka in Japan and Dr James Thomson in the USA, "reprogramme" human skin cells to make them act like embryonic stem cells.

Find out more

Books

Illustrated Dictionary of Biology (Usborne Publishing, 2006)

New Technology: Medical Technology, Robert Snedden (Evans Books, 2008)

Science at the Edge: Frontiers of Surgery, Ann Fullick (Heinemann Library, 2009)

Science at the Edge: Organ Transplantation, Ann Fullick (Heinemann Library, 2009)

Websites

http://americanhistory.si.edu/anatomy/bodyparts/nma03_bodyparts.html
Find out more about body organs with this interactive guide.

www.bbc.co.uk/science/humanbody/body/interactives/3djigsaw_02/index.shtml?organs
Another way to find out more about the body's organs.

www.mayoclinic.com/health/coronary-angioplasty/MM00048
Watch an animation showing what happens in a coronary angioplasty operation.

www.pbs.org/wgbh/nova/eheart/transplantwave.html
Do your own heart transplant! With this hands-on guide you can saw through the ribs, cut out the old heart, and sew in a new one.

www.tellmeaboutstemcells.org/index.php
Read this simple but useful guide to stem cell basics.

www.wtgf.org
Find out about events, winners, and stories from the World Transplant Games.

Topics to research

- Research a body system. Pick one of the major body systems and do some research into it. Which organs are involved? What do they do, and how do they work together? What are the connections to other organ systems?

- Find out about transplants in your area. Do they do transplants in your local hospital? If not, where would you have to go for a kidney transplant? What about other transplants?

- What are the rules about stem cell research in your country? Find out what the law is and who regulates research into stem cells.

- Who is doing transplant or stem cell research? Find out about some research projects in your country involving transplants or stem cells.

Glossary

amputee   someone who has had a limb removed

anaemia   reduced numbers of red blood cells in the blood

anaesthetized   put to sleep with drugs that block pain

angioplasty   operation for unblocking blood vessels

antibiotics   chemical substances that can fight off and kill bacteria

antibodies   substances found in blood that can destroy bacteria

cartilage   tough, springy material that forms some parts of the skeleton

cell culture   cells grown in the laboratory by feeding them the correct mixture of nutrients and other chemicals

connective tissue   bone, tendons, ligaments, blood, and other tissues involved in the structure of the body

cornea   surface of the eye

diabetes   illness in which the body cannot control levels of sugar in the blood properly

differentiate   become specialized for a particular job

dormant   inactive

electrode   electrical connection

embryo   baby in the early stages of its development in the mother's womb

epithelium   type of tissue that forms thin sheets of cells

gene   section of DNA; the way that characteristics are passed on from one generation to the next. Genes are found in the nucleus of the cell.

genetics   the study of genes and the way they work

hormone   substance that acts as a signal or control, which is produced in one place and travels through the blood to one or more target areas

immune system   the body's defences against disease

infection   when bacteria or other microbes get into the body and cause illness

insulin   hormone involved in controlling blood sugar levels. People with diabetes do not have enough insulin.

lubricated   oiled

mitosis   when cells divide in two

mucus   slimy, sticky liquid that lines parts of the body

nutrient   substance that the body needs to work properly, which comes from the breakdown of food

pericardium   tough double membrane that protects the heart and helps to hold it in place

radiation   rays or waves of energy

radiotherapy   use of high-energy radiation to kill cancer cells

stem cells   non-specialized cells in the body that can divide, and can also turn into one or more kinds of specialized cell

stroke   when the blood supply to part of the brain is blocked and damage is caused to brain cells

tissue   group of cells that are all of the same type, or of two or three related types

tumour   group of cancer cells

turbine   many-bladed fan or propeller

unethical   not morally correct

ventricles   the two large chambers that contract to push blood out of the heart

virus   tiny biological particle that can reproduce itself inside living cells

XLP   (X-linked lymphoproliferative syndrome, or Duncan's disease) very rare hereditary disease found only in boys, in which the immune system reacts abnormally to infection

Index